American Holidays / Celebraciones en los Estados Unidos

MEMORIAL DAY
DÍA DE LOS CAÍDOS

Connor Dayton Traducción al español: Eduardo Alamán

PowerKiDS press™

New York

Published in 2012 by The Rosen Publishing Group, Inc.
29 East 21st Street, New York, NY 10010

First Edition

Editor: Jennifer Way
Book Design: Julio Gil

Traducción al español: Eduardo Alamán

Photo Credits: Cover, p. 23 Ariel Skelley/age fotostock; pp. 4–5 © www.iStockphoto.com/Eileen Hart; pp. 7, 9, 19, 24 (top right) Shutterstock.com; pp. 11, 24 (top left) Mark Wilson/Getty Images; pp. 13, 24 (bottom right) Joshua Roberts-Pool/Getty Images; p. 15 Kris Connor/Getty Images; pp. 17, 24 (bottom left) Tim Yuan/Shutterstock.com; pp. 20–21 Robert Laberge/Getty Images.

Library of Congress Cataloging-in-Publication Data

Dayton, Connor.
 [Memorial Day. Spanish & English]
 Memorial Day = Día de los caídos / by Connor Dayton. — 1st ed.
     p. cm. — (American holidays = Celebraciones en los Estados Unidos)
 Includes index.
 ISBN 978-1-4488-6709-7 (library binding)
 1. Memorial Day—Juvenile literature. I. Title. II. Title: Día de los caídos.
 E642.D3918 2012
 394.262—dc23
                                    2011024111

Web Sites: Due to the changing nature of Internet links, PowerKids Press has developed an online list of Web sites related to the subject of this book. This site is updated regularly. Please use this link to access the list: www.powerkidslinks.com/amh/memorial/

Manufactured in the United States of America

CPSIA Compliance Information: Batch #WW12PK: For Further Information contact Rosen Publishing, New York, New York at 1-800-237-9932

Contents

Contenido

Memorial Day is the last Monday in May.

El Día de los Caídos se celebra el último lunes de mayo.

This holiday honors soldiers who died serving America.

Esta celebración honra a los soldados que han muerto sirviendo a los Estados Unidos.

Flags fly at **half-staff** on Memorial Day morning. This is done for fallen soldiers.

Las banderas ondean a **media asta** este día. Así se honra a los soldados que han perdido la vida.

People visit graves on Memorial Day.

Las personas visitan tumbas el Día de los Caídos.

11

The president places a **wreath** at Arlington National **Cemetery**, in Virginia.

El presidente coloca una **corona de flores** en el **Cementerio** Nacional de Arlington, en Virginia.

The National Memorial Day Concert is in Washington, D.C.

El concierto que celebra el Día de los Caídos se lleva a cabo en Washington, D.C.

Cities have Memorial Day **parades**.

Las ciudades celebran el Día de los Caídos con **desfiles**.

Families have Memorial
Day picnics.

Muchas familias organizan
picnics este día.

The Indianapolis 500 is held on Memorial Day. This is a big car race.

La carrera de las 500 Millas de Indianapolis se realiza este día.

Memorial Day is the start of summer fun!

¡El Día de los Caídos nos recuerda que el verano está por comenzar!

Words to Know / Palabras que debes saber

cemetery / (el) cementerio

half-staff / media asta

parade / (el) desfile

wreath / (la) corona de flores

Index

Índice